Picture the Past
Life in a California Mission

Sally Senzell Isaacs

Heinemann Library
Chicago, Illinois

© 2002 Reed Educational & Professional Publishing
Published by Heinemann Library,
an imprint of Reed Educational & Professional Publishing,
Chicago, IL
Customer Service 888-454-2279
Visit our website at www.heinemannlibrary.com

Produced for Heinemann Library by
   Bender Richardson White.
Editor: Lionel Bender
Designer and Media Conversion: Ben White
Picture Researcher: Cathy Stastny
Production Controller: Kim Richardson

0908
10 9 8 7

Printed in China

Library of Congress Cataloging-in-Publication Data.
Isaacs, Sally Senzell, 1950-
   Life in a California mission / Sally Senzell Isaacs.
      p. cm. -- (Picture the past)
   Includes bibliographical references and index.
   ISBN 1-58810-249-1 (hb.bdg.) ISBN 1-58810-414-1 (pbk.
bdg.)
   ISBN 978-1-58810-249-2(HC) ISBN 978-1-58810-414-4(pbk)
   1. California--History--To 1846--Juvenile literature.
2. Missions, Spanish--California--History--Juvenile
literature. 3. California--Social life and customs--18th
century--Juvenile literature. 4. California--Social life and
customs--19th century--Juvenile literature. 5. Indians of
North America--Missions--California--Juvenile literature. (1.
Missions--California--History.) I. Title.
   F864 .I83 2001
   979.4--dc21
                              2001000496

Special thanks to Mike Carpenter and Scott Westerfield
at Heinemann Library for editorial and design guidance
and direction.

Acknowledgments
The producers and publishers are grateful to the follow-
ing for permission to reproduce copyright material:
Morton Beebe, S.F./Corbis Images: page 30. Craig
Aurness/Corbis Images: page 17. Richard Cummins/
Corbis Images: pages 3, 12, 19. Lowell Georgia/Corbis
Images: page 11. North Wind Pictures: pages 1, 14-15,
16, 23, 25, 26. Peter Newark's American Pictures: pages
8, 9, 10, 13, 18, 21. Werner Forman Photos/Field Museum
of Natural History, Chicago: page 7.
Cover photograph: Peter Newark's American Pictures.

Illustrations by John James, pages 6, 14, 22, 24, 27, 29;
Mark Bergin, page 20; Gerald Wood, page 28.
Map by Stefan Chabluk.
Cover make-up: Mike Pilley, Radius.

Note to the Reader
Some words are shown in bold, **like
this.** You can find out what they mean
by looking in the glossary.

ABOUT THIS BOOK

This book tells about daily life in California missions from 1769 to 1823. During these years, the leaders of Spain sent **priest**s to California to set up **communities** called missions. Spain wanted to create colonies in California to stop other countries from owning land there.

The priests had two goals: to build missions for Spain and to teach the **Roman Catholic religion** and Spanish ways to **Native Americans.** We have illustrated the book with paintings and drawings from mission times and with artists' ideas of how things looked in the missions. We also include modern photographs of missions.

The Author

Sally Senzell Isaacs is a professional writer and editor of nonfiction books for children. She graduated from Indiana University, earning a B.S. degree in Education with majors in American History and Sociology. For some years, she was the Editorial Director of Reader's Digest Educational Division. Sally Senzell Isaacs lives in New Jersey with her husband and two children.

CONTENTS

Wanted: California 4
First People 6
Spain Moves In 8
The Royal Road 10
Beads and Bells 12
The Mission 14
Mission Buildings............ 16
Priests and Church 18
Spanish Soldiers............ 20
A Day's Work 22
Growing Food.................. 24
Meals and Recipes 26
End of the Missions...... 28
Missions Today 30
Glossary............................ 31
More Books to Read...... 31
Index.............................. 32

Wanted: California

In the 1500s, Spain owned land all over the world. In North America, Spain owned land in what is now Florida, Georgia, Arizona, Texas, and New Mexico. The country we call Mexico belonged to Spain, too.

In the 1700s, Spain's leaders wanted to own land in what is now called California. They decided to set up missions there. A mission is a **community** run by teachers of **religion.** To quickly get people to live in their communities, Spain planned to have **Native Americans** move in.

Look for these
The illustration of a mission boy and girl shows you the subject of each double-page story in the book.

The picture of a mission bell marks boxes with interesting facts about mission life.

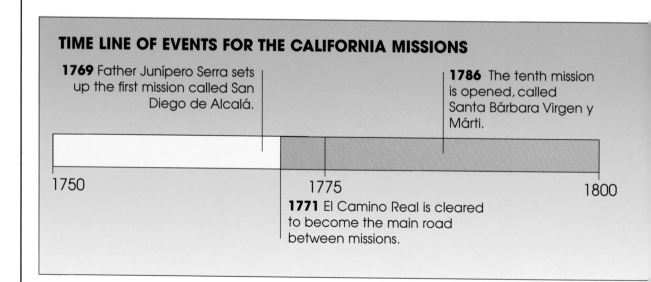

TIME LINE OF EVENTS FOR THE CALIFORNIA MISSIONS

1769 Father Junípero Serra sets up the first mission called San Diego de Alcalá.

1786 The tenth mission is opened, called Santa Bárbara Virgen y Márti.

1750

1775

1800

1771 El Camino Real is cleared to become the main road between missions.

In 54 years, Spain set up 21 missions in California. A dirt road called El Camino Real connected the missions. Supplies, soldiers, and **missionaries** traveled from Mexico by ship and on foot.

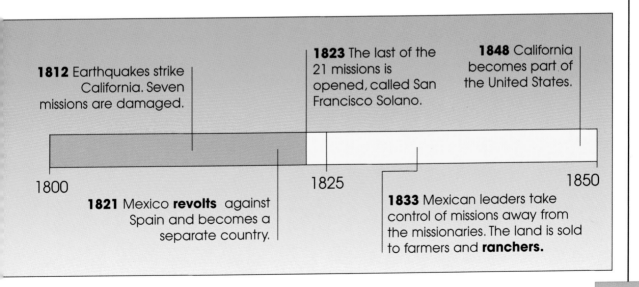

1812 Earthquakes strike California. Seven missions are damaged.

1823 The last of the 21 missions is opened, called San Francisco Solano.

1848 California becomes part of the United States.

1800

1825

1850

1821 Mexico **revolts** against Spain and becomes a separate country.

1833 Mexican leaders take control of missions away from the missionaries. The land is sold to farmers and **ranchers.**

First People

For thousands of years, **Native Americans** lived on the land we now call California. They fished in the ocean and streams. They hunted small animals with bows and arrows. They gathered wild nuts and berries to eat. In most parts of California, Native Americans did not have to clear fields and plant seeds. It was easy to find food.

The men of this Pomo village are building a home with tall grass. The women are pressing acorns into flour. They will use the flour to make bread.

The Native Americans had **respect** for everything in nature. That was part of their **religion.** The streams, trees, sky, and animals were all part of the most important god, Great Spirit. The people showed their respect in their songs, their celebrations, and their art.

The Native Americans made baskets out of grass. The baskets were strong enough to hold water or acorn soup. Baskets were also used as hats and baby carriers.

NATIVE AMERICAN GROUPS

About 300 thousand Native Americans lived in California. They lived in large groups. Among the groups that lived near the California missions were the Pomo, Miwok, Ohlone, Chumash, Tongva, Serrano, Kitanemuk, Monache, Salinan, Nisenan, Yokuts, Esselen.

SPECIAL TREATS

Acorns—the nuts of oak trees—could be found everywhere. Most meals included acorns. For special meals, the people enjoyed eating insects, especially grasshoppers.

Spain Moves In

THE PRIESTS

Father Serra was a **missionary** priest for the **Roman Catholic** Church. A missionary is a person who is sent by a church to convince people to choose that church's **religion.** Roman Catholic missionaries wanted the Native Americans to follow the teachings of the Bible and to believe in one God.

Around 1760, Spain wanted to build **communities** north of Mexico, in California. Spain's leaders wanted Spanish people to move from Mexico into the new California communities.

But there were not enough people who wanted to go. So the leaders asked **priests** to build communities called missions and move **Native Americans** into the missions. The priests would teach the Native Americans a new way to live, work, and pray.

The Spanish priests wanted to **convert** the Native Americans. People who convert give up their own religion and accept another. The Native Americans would become Roman Catholic.

In 1769, a priest named Father Junípero Serra rode a mule from Mexico into the area we now call San Diego, California. He brought with him soldiers, priests, and builders. Their job was to build a mission. They hoped that some day the mission would grow into a town, called a *pueblo* in Spanish.

GOOD OR BAD?

The priests thought missions were helpful to Spain and to the Native Americans. But life became worse for some Native Americans. They had to leave home, give up their beliefs, speak a new language, and work without pay.

Father Serra and his helpers arrived near present-day San Diego, California, in July 1769. They climbed to the top of a hill and planted a large wooden cross. They would build the mission on this land.

The Royal Road

By 1772, Spanish **missionaries** had started five missions. In 1781, there were thirteen missions. By 1823, 21 missions stretched along California's west coast.

A single road connected the missions. It was called El Camino Real, which means "the royal road." A traveler could walk from one mission to the next in one day.

Missionaries, soldiers, and other people used El Camino Real to take supplies to the new missions. They also took food grown on the missions to the soldiers living in nearby forts, or **presidios.**

El Camino Real started as a foot trail through the grass and trees. As missions grew, small towns, called pueblos, also grew nearby. The narrow trail became a wider road. By the time California became part of the United States in 1848, stagecoaches were rumbling along the road. Today U.S. Highway 101 closely follows El Camino Real.

El Camino Real stretched 530 miles (853 kilometers) through California, from San Diego to Sonoma, just north of San Francisco. It was part of a Spanish trail leading from Mission San Antonio in Texas to California. This is a sign for El Camino Real.

KING'S HIGHWAY
CAMINO REAL
OLD SAN ANTONIO ROAD
MARKED BY THE
DAUGHTERS OF THE
AMERICAN REVOLUTION
AND THE STATE OF TEXAS
A.D. 1918

Beads and Bells

As the Spanish people began to build a mission, some **Native Americans** wandered over to watch. They lived in villages nearby. The **missionaries** offered them glass beads as gifts in exchange for help with the building. They also offered the Native Americans food, clothes, and a place to live. Some Native Americans wanted to stay on the mission. Others did not want to. Sometimes Spanish soldiers forced them to stay.

A bell was one of the first things placed in the mission. Many Native Americans came to find out what made the strange sound.

The missionaries wanted to **convert** the Native Americans. Many Native Americans agreed to convert. Then they were called **neophytes.**

Many neophytes were soon sorry that they moved to the mission. Soldiers would not let them leave without permission. They were forced to wake up early and work hard. They missed their villages and families. Many got sick and died from such diseases as smallpox carried by the Spanish people.

THE BELLS

The mission bell told many messages:
- It is time to pray.
- It is time to go to work.
- Get ready for a party.
- A stranger is coming.
- Someone has died.
- The day's work is done.

These two **priests** taught prayers and farming skills to local people at the mission at Santa Barbara around 1910. They are dressed just as the priests would have done in the late-1700s.

13

The Mission

A mission was something like a small town. There was a church, workshops, a kitchen, and a dining room. There were sleeping rooms for the **priests,** soldiers, and **neophytes.** Some missions allowed the neophytes to leave at night. Some forced the neophytes to live inside the mission. The priests were afraid that they would never return once they went home.

Most missions were built in the shape of a four-sided **quadrangle.** Outside the quadrangle, there were fields for growing **crops.** There were also fenced-in areas for farm animals.

Many neophytes hated the strict rules of the mission. They hated being punished when soldiers said they did not work hard enough.

Many neophytes ran away. Some went back to their villages and asked their friends to help them attack the mission. This was called a **revolt**. Some neophytes were caught.

On this mission, neophytes are making rope and baskets.

Mission Buildings

Before they built the mission, the **priests** put up a small hut of branches. This was their church until the buildings were finished. **Native Americans** worked hard to build the mission. Many of them knew how to carve and paint beautifully. Many mission churches had walls and ceilings with colorful pictures made by Native Americans.

ADOBE

Many mission buildings were made of **adobe.** This is a mixture of clay, straw, and water. The mixture was poured into brick shapes and placed in the sun to bake. Children stood by the drying bricks and kept wandering animals away.

This is Mission Santa Bárbara Virgen y Mártir. The roof is made of bricklike tiles. Early mission buildings had straw roofs.

Each mission priest lived in a small room with a bed, table, and candles for light. Most mission furniture was made of wood by the neophytes.

A priest, some Spanish workers, and many **neophytes** lived in the mission. In some missions, neophyte girls and unmarried women stayed together in one large room. Young boys stayed in another. Married couples lived in small houses outside the **quadrangle.** A few soldiers shared one of the mission rooms. Most soldiers lived at the nearby **presidio.**

EARTH-QUAKES

During December 1812, several earthquakes shook California. The buildings in seven missions were badly damaged.

Priests and Church

The **priests** expected the **neophytes** to go to church services every day. The priests taught them to sing prayers in **Latin** and Spanish.

The neophytes did not understand the words. Some enjoyed the tunes. Others sang because they knew that neophytes who did not learn the songs were whipped or made to work harder.

FORGET THE PAST

In the mission, neophytes were not allowed to pray to their **Native American** gods. Sometimes they secretly ran back to their villages for special celebrations. In 1824, there were more than 20,000 **Roman Catholic** Native Americans in California.

As church services began, everyone kneeled in front of the cross.

The priests believed they were helping the Native Americans by teaching them prayers and skills. Some priests tried to learn Native American languages. One priest wrote a 400 page book of Native American words. It helped him teach his lessons. Many neophytes learned to speak Spanish.

Some churches were beautifully decorated inside and had wooden benches for people to sit on during services. Others had no chairs.

Spanish Soldiers

Some soldiers were very cruel to the **neophytes.** They made them work hard in the fields near the mission.

Some mission soldiers believed that **Native Americans** should be punished if they did not work hard and change their ways. Soldiers also knew that many Native Americans were angry about the way missions treated them. Soldiers tried to protect the **priests** and other Spanish **settlers** from **revolts.**

Most soldiers lived in a **presidio.** A presidio had high walls to protect the soldiers and their guns. There were four presidios in California—at San Diego, Santa Barbara, Monterey, and San Francisco.

The soldiers traveled back and forth to the missions. They wore thick leather jackets so that Native American arrows could not harm them.

Soldiers and priests are riding away from the mission at San Carlos de Borromeo de Carmelo.

21

A Day's Work

Clang! Clang! This was the first sound in the mission each morning. As the sun rose in the sky, a **priest** rang a bell, and everyone hurried to the church. After saying prayers, people walked to the dining room for a breakfast of cereal. Then they went to work.

The mission was a busy place. The priests hoped that some day the Native Americans would turn the mission land into a real town. This did not happen.

Some **neophytes** taught others. Teenagers were taught to plant and build things. Younger children gathered firewood, picked olives, and chased away birds.

WHAT NEOPHYTES LEARNED

Men and boys made
- leather saddles and shoes
- **adobe** bricks
- iron tools
- furniture

Girls and women made
- cloth
- soap
- pottery
- candles

SUNRISE TO SUNSET

5:00 A.M. Wake up
5:30 A.M. Church services and breakfast
6:00 A.M. Work
12:00 NOON Eat lunch and rest
2:00 P.M. Work
5:00 P.M. Eat dinner
6:00 P.M. Lessons in **religion**
9:00 or 10:00 P.M. To bed

Mission life was very different from life in the **Native American** villages. At the mission, the Native Americans did not have to worry about finding food for their next meal. However, many of them missed their freedom and did not like rules and schedules. Many were unhappy in the missions.

Growing Food

Neophytes worked very hard in the mission fields. They cleared trees from the land. They planted seedlings for growing wheat, barley, beans, and corn. They dug small ditches so that water could run from the streams to the fields. Many missions had orchards filled with olive, apple, and pear trees. Many had gardens filled with grape vines.

SLAVES

While **Native Americans** were building missions, African men and women were working in cotton fields in the southern United States. Both groups worked for no pay and had no freedom. This was called slavery.

A **priest** tells neophytes where to dig ditches and plant seedlings.

Stacks of wheat, gallons of olive oil, and barrels of wine were produced at the missions. Most were sent to the **presidio** and to nearby towns. Some were put on ships and sold in cities in the eastern United States and in other countries. The missions earned money by selling these products. The neophytes earned no money for all their work.

MISSION ANIMALS

All the missions raised animals. Cows provided food, leather, and candle wax. Horses and oxen pulled carts and plows. Sheep's wool was made into blankets and clothes.

Oxen pulled wooden carts, called *carretas*. People rode and goods were carried on the cart.

Meals and Recipes

The **neophyte** girls and women cooked and made meals for everyone in the mission. They followed recipes from Mexico. Sometimes they cooked beef and corn together into a soup called *pozole.* Sometimes they baked flat breads, called *tortillas,* and filled them with meat.

The first orange trees in California came from the Spanish missions in the late 1700s. Except for Florida, California now grows more oranges than any other state.

Mission Recipe – Jiricalla

Here is a recipe for one of the sweet dishes prepared in some missions. In Spanish, it is called *jiricalla*.

WARNING: Do not cook anything unless there is an adult to help you. Always ask an adult to help you use a beater, cook at the stove, and to handle hot liquids.

YOU WILL NEED
3 eggs
2 cups (480 ml) milk
1/2 cup (120 g) sugar
dash of nutmeg
3 tablespoons cornstarch
1/4 cup (40 ml) water

FOLLOW THE STEPS

1. Preheat the oven to 375° Fahrenheit (190°Centigrade).
2. Crack the eggs and place the yolks in one bowl and the whites in another bowl. Beat the yolks with a fork.
3. Put the milk in a pan and cook it until just before it boils.
4. Add the sugar and nutmeg.

5. Slowly stir in the beaten egg yolks.
6. Add the water to the cornstarch and stir until it is completely mixed. Add this to the milk-egg mixture in the pan.
7. Stir the mixture while cooking over medium heat until it becomes thick. Pour it into a small pan or

bowl that can be heated in an oven.
8. Use a beater to beat the egg whites until they are light and fluffy. Spoon on top of the custard. Sprinkle some sugar on top.
9. Heat in the oven about 10 minutes or until the top is golden brown. Cool before eating.

End of the Missions

In the 1830s, people from all over the world were moving to California for its good weather and good land. People from other parts of the United States were heading to California, too. The Mexican leaders did not want people from other countries to take over California. They decided to sell the rich mission land to Mexican farmers and **ranchers.** They closed most of the mission buildings.

LOST LIVES

Before the missions, there were about 340 thousand **Native Americans** in California. By 1840, there were only 100 thousand. In 1859, there were 30 thousand.

Many Native Americans took jobs on the new farms and **ranches.** They were often paid very little. Sometimes they were treated badly.

When the missions closed, the Mexican leaders promised to give the **neophytes** land and farm animals. But the leaders broke these promises. If neophytes did get land, **settlers** soon took the land away from them.

In 1848, the United States fought a war against Mexico and won California. That same year, gold was found there. Over the next two years, 85,000 people moved to California. Many Native Americans were killed by gold miners, eager to dig up the land and get rich.

The neophytes could not go back to their old villages. Settlers took over that land, too. Native American life would never be the same as it was before the missions began.

Missions Today

The mission buildings sat empty and broken for many years. Then, in the 1900s, people living near the missions began to rebuild the churches and some other buildings. Artists and builders studied pictures of the old buildings. They made the new buildings look just like the old ones. Now all the missions are open for visitors. Services are held in most of the churches.

The city of San Francisco grew up around Mission San Francisco de Asís. As in many of the missions, the old church is now surrounded by modern buildings.

Glossary

adobe bricklike material made of clay, straw, and water

community group of people who live in the same area and live by the same laws

convert change from one religion to another

crop plant grown to provide food

Latin main language of Ancient Romans that was once used by the Roman Catholic Church

missionary person who is sent by a religious group to convince people to choose that group's religion

Native American member of one of the first groups of people to live in North and South America

neophyte Native American living inside a mission who has changed his or her religion to become Catholic

oxen strong animals, related to cows

presidio strong building where Spanish soldiers lived and protected the people around them

priest in certain religions, someone who can lead services and perform ceremonies.

quadrangle closed shape with four sides

ranch large farm for cattle, horses, or sheep. Someone who owns a ranch is called a rancher

Roman Catholic belonging to the religion whose leader is the pope

religion system of belief in God or gods, faith, and prayer

respect admire and treat with kindness

revolt fight against people in charge of a place

settler person who makes a new home in a new place

More Books to Read

Kalman, Bobbie, and Greg Nickles. *Spanish Missions.* New York: Crabtree Publishing Company, 1996.

The Missions of California 21-volume series exploring California's Mission era. New York: Rosen Publishing Group, 2000.

Index

animals 6, 7, 14, 16, 23, 25, 29

bells 4, 12, 13, 22
builders and buildings 9, 12, 14, 16–17, 24, 28, 30

California 4, 5, 6, 7, 8, 9, 10, 11, 18, 26, 28, 29
children 16, 23, 26
churches 8, 14, 16, 18–19, 22, 23, 30

El Camino Real 4, 5, 10, 11

farming and fields 13, 14, 20, 24, 28, 29
Florida 4, 26
food 6, 7, 10, 12, 22, 23, 24–25, 26, 27
furniture 17, 19, 23

language 9, 18, 19

Mexico and Mexican people 4, 5, 8, 9, 26, 28, 29
missionaries 5, 8, 10

Monterey 21

Native Americans 6, 7, 8, 9, 12, 13, 16, 18, 19, 20, 22, 23, 24, 28, 29
neophytes 13, 14, 15, 17, 18, 23, 24, 25, 26, 29

pray and prayers 8, 13, 18, 19, 22
presidios (forts) 10, 17, 21, 25
priests 8, 9, 13, 14, 16, 17, 18–19, 20, 21, 22, 24
pueblos (towns) 9, 11, 14, 22, 25
punishment 15, 18

ranchers 5, 28
religion 4, 7, 8, 23
revolts 5, 15, 20
Roman Catholics 8, 18

San Francisco 11, 21, 30
Santa Barbara 4, 16, 21

Serra, Father Junípero 4, 8, 9
settlers 20, 29
sickness and diseases 13
singing and songs 7, 18
slaves 24
sleeping rooms 14, 17
soldiers 5, 9, 10, 12, 13, 14, 15, 17, 20–21
Spain and Spanish people 4, 5, 8, 9, 10, 11, 12, 13, 20, 26, 27

teachers and teaching 4, 8, 18, 19, 22
Texas 4, 11

United States 5, 11, 24, 25, 28, 29

villages 6, 12, 13, 15, 18, 23, 29

work 8, 9, 13, 15, 16, 17, 18, 20, 22–23, 24, 25, 28